SMILE AND OTHER STORIES

DEEPA

Copyright © Deepa
All Rights Reserved.

She dedicate this book to his son

D.Lithin

Contents

Author Profile

V. DEEPA M.A., M.Phil., M.Ed., NET

She was born on 07th July 1987 in Karur, Tamilnadu. Her qualification is M.A., M.Phil., M.Ed., NET. She has cracked NET Exam in 2018. She is Passionate towards Literature and Short Story. This is the first Step of her writing career with the constant support of her husband and family. Currently she is working as an Assistant Professor of English, Velammal Institute of Technology, Chennai.

ACKNOWLEDGEMENTS

The Author wish to express her gratitude to her Life Partner Mr.S.Deepan M.A., M.Phil., B.Ed., NET for his constant support and Guidance in all her endeavours.

PROLOGUE

Short Stories can be easily read and understand by everyone. These stories are for the beginners who can start reading books and learn the basic principles of life.

Smile Gives a New Wake Up

A father named Lokesh is very fond of her daughter Pooja. He prefers to play and chat with her after returning home from the office. He spends his days more happily. Once an emergency occurs that means a new project task is assigned to him. He is doing many practices and homework, but he couldn't get success in his new task. Due to the busy schedule, he is working overtime in the office and coming home very late and he was not able to spend his time with her daughter. He could not be able to find a solution. Something is missing in his attitude and it makes him stressed and fallen sick under depression. The next day he could not go to the office as his fever raised to the level of 103 degrees. When *he was lying in a bed his daughter came to him and said Daddy, Smile Please. At that moment, he realised the thing that he has forgotten his SMILE and also his daughter's smile. He started smiling at her daughter and she also replied an answer to his big question of missing attitude with a little and adorable smile. Mr Lokesh emerged from his downturn and on the following day, he completed his work and promoted as a Managing Director of the new branch established by his Organization.*

Moral: Smile Boosts the Man's Ability

II

Smile Adores Confidence

Once a boy challenged his classmate that he will perform well in Cricket annual sports meet. He didn't have any idea to play cricket. He Came home and told his mother about his challenge and also his fear. His mother encouraged him with a smile. His mother gave few plans to practice cricket. Then his mother arranged a coach for him and took him day by day with a smile. The boy couldn't adapt to the practices given by the coach, yet his mom consistently greeted him with a smile. The boy asked his mother, how you are welcoming me with a smile when I can't meet the expectation. The mother answered that Participation is superior to winning. The mother supported the boy with a smile that you are attempting to

play cricket to keep up his promise. That's the spirit that is needed for winning. If you keeping on trying your goal you will achieve it. The boy said mom that your smile gives confidence to me. The mother boosted the boy daily with her smile. The boy started to realise his position and treats the sport seriously and practised well to play in the annual sports Cricket. On the sports day, the mother came to the stadium to encourage her son with a smile. The moment he saw her mother with a smile, he gains confidence and dominated the match and beats his rival in the challenge. After winning the competition, the boy said smile leads to the path of success.

Moral: Smile can gain confidence.

III

The Red and Blue Coat

Once, there were two boys who were the best friends. They wanted to stay as best friends forever and were determined not to let anything spoil their friendship. They grew up together and later, married and had their own families. They even built houses that faced each other. There was also a narrow path that they created which acted as a border separating their farms. One day, a man from their village thought of playing a trick on them. He found a double colored coat from a local tailor and dressed himself in that. "The coat was BLUE on one side and RED on the other".

The next day, the man wore the coat and started walking along the small path between the houses of the two friends. He made some loud noises so that he could catch the attention of both the boys who were working on their respective farms. In the evening, when the friends sat down for tea, they had a little chat among themselves. "Wasn't that red coat that the man was wearing in the morning, lovely? The first friend asked.

"It is a blue coat, not a red one", the other friend said confidently.

"I saw him from very close and he was wearing a lovely red coat", the first one said.

"No you are wrong. It was a blue coat". The second one replied.

"You are mistaken. It was a red coat", the first one insisted.

This argument continued for a while until it changed into a fight. The two men started insulting each other; they fell on the ground, hit each other and started screaming; "OUR FRIENDSHIP IS OVER NOW". Right then, the who had played the trick on them, was passing by. He took out the coat, which was the fight, and showed to them. The boys realized that the coat was indeed blue one side and red from the other. "We have been friends for all our lives and you have spoilt our friendship. It is entirely your fault", both the friends blamed the trick.

"Please don't blame me for all this", the man said, "I am not the reason behind your fight. Both of you were right and wrong at the same time about the coat, as both of you saw it from your own point of view".

MORAL: "EVERYONE HAS A DIFFERENT OPINION".

He attempted to the cows however he got a decent kick. Then, at that point, he went to the pig. It hit his head .He neglect to take care of the hen. His child was cry until rani got back he neglected to get ready nourishment for his child.

On the evening, the spouse returned home from the field. Rani completed all her field work totally there is no need of his help in work. She got back yet subu would not satisfy in his work and furthermore with the assistance of Madhu he would not capable no complete her work. He acknowledged his failure and hung down his head in disgrace. There after he didn't find fault with his wife down . They lived cheerfully for quite a while.

Moral : Don't Find Fault with anyone.